"D.B. Gilles has discovered the eerie correspondences among the 12 stages of the Hero's Journey, the 12 steps of AA recovery, and the sometimes challenging experience of becoming a professional writer. In his earthy, human and extremely lucid style, he spells out how you can find much greater satisfaction and success in your writing through a 12-step approach. It's a must-read for writers who struggle with their art, which would be all of us."

— Christopher Vogler, author, *The Writer's Journey*

"Everyone I know respects D.B. Gilles as a writer, teacher, and critic. In *Writers Rehab*, D.B. has written a great book about my life — how I could've written *Lord of the Rings* if I only had the time. But thanks to this 12-step book, I'll stop telling people I did and face the music, day after tomorrow the latest."

— Charlie Rubin, screenwriter; *Seinfeld*, *In Living Color*, *Law & Order: Criminal Intent*

"Trust me, there isn't a writer alive — a veteran or a newcomer — who hasn't had to wrestle with the inner demons that D.B. Gilles neatly identifies, skewers, and exorcises in this compact but indispensable book. We writers are a highly neurotic and fragile bunch, and we need all the help we can get!"

— Robert Masello, bestselling author, *The Romanov Cross*

"*Writers Rehab* takes a clever premise and uses it to deliver surprising amounts of wisdom, support and guidance, to writers of all stripes."

— Dennis Palumbo, psychotherapist and author; co-writer of *My Favorite Year*

"D.B. Gilles offers tough, practical advice about the craft of writing. He gives a loving kick in the ass to help get the writer started and encouragement to keep the writer on track throughout the creative process. He identifies the many hurdles a writer faces and offers solutions to overcome those hurdles."

— Matt Williams, creator, *Rosanne*; co-creator, *Home Improvement*

WRITERS REHAB

A 12-STEP PROGRAM
FOR WRITERS
WHO CAN'T GET
THEIR ACTS TOGETHER

D.B. GILLES

Published by Michael Wiese Productions
12400 Ventura Blvd. #1111
Studio City, CA 91604
tel. 818.379.8799
fax 818.986.3408
mw@mwp.com
www.mwp.com

Cover design: Johnny Ink www.johnnyink.com
Book design: Gina Mansfield Design
Copy editor: David Wright

Printed by McNaughton & Gunn, Inc., Saline, Michigan
Manufactured in the United States of America

© 2013 by D.B. Gilles

Library of Congress Cataloging-in-Publication Data

Gilles, D. B.
 Writer's rehab : a 12-step program for writers who can't get their
acts together / D.B. Gilles.
     pages cm
 ISBN 978-1-61593-156-9 (pbk.)
 1. Motion picture authorship. 2. Television authorship. 3. Twelve-
step programs. 4. Writer's block. I. Title.
 PN1996.G445 2013
 808.2'3--dc23

                                    2013016169

Printed on recycled stock
Publisher plants ten trees for every one tree used to produce this book.

Also by D.B. Gilles

FICTION

I Hate My Book Club

Colder Than Death

NON-FICTION

*The Screenwriter Within:
New Strategies to Finish Your
Screenplay & Get a Deal*

*You're Funny!
Turn Your Sense of Humor
into a Lucrative New Career*

The Portable Film School

PLAYS

Inadmissible

Sparkling Object

Cash Flow

Men's Singles

The Legendary Stardust Boys

The Girl Who Loved the Beatles

HUMOR

W. The First 100 Days: A White House Journal
(with Sheldon Woodbury)

SPECIAL ACKNOWLEDGMENT

Jane Dystel.
For her support over the last 15 years.

DEDICATION

There's a Chinese proverb I like:
Teachers open the door,
but you must enter by yourself.

To every student I've worked with,
either in a classroom, in person,
by phone, or e-mail,
I dedicate this book to you.

SPECIAL DEDICATION

For Jane Terese Campbell,
who helped me through
the dark places into the light.

Being entirely honest with oneself is a good exercise.

SIGMUND FREUD

table of
Contents

How *Writers Rehab* Can Work Best for You   xiv

Introduction
Writers on the Verge   xi

STEP 1 | You admitted you were powerless over   1
             your inability to write and that your
             writing life had become unmanageable.

             It's Time to Stop Bullshitting Yourself   2

STEP 2 | You came to believe that a Power greater   11
             than yourself could restore you to
             help you regain control of that plot that
             wouldn't bend.

             We Want What We Want When We Want It   12

STEP 3 | You made a decision to turn your clichéd,   19
             underdeveloped protagonists and
             meandering subplots over to the care of
             God and a firm grasp of the 3-Act structure
             as you understood Him and it.

             If You Want to Drown, Why Torture
             Yourself by Swimming in Shallow Water?   20

STEP 4 | You made a searching and fearless moral   29
inventory of the troublesome 256-page
romantic subplot you thought would add a
magical realism to your bloated 981-page first
draft that didn't get started until page 189.

Scared Money Never Wins   30

STEP 5 | Admitted to God, to yourself, and to   41
another human being the exact nature of
your inability to stick to a project once
you've begun without throwing in the towel
and starting something new only to give
up on that one too.

Don't Be an 80-Percenter   42

STEP 6 | You're entirely ready to have God help you   47
create complex characters who resemble
three-dimensional human beings rather
than trite, shallow, stick figure characters
we've seen a million times before.

**Disappointment and Anxiety Are
Messengers Saying You Are Headed
for Unknown Territory**   48

STEP 7 | Humbly asked God to remove your   59
shortcomings, especially with regard to
your inability to take criticism, to lose
your ego, and to confront the deep-seated
problems of what you've written.

Lose the Attitude, Ego & Superiority Complex 60

STEP 8 | You listed all the people you had 69
harmed by asking them to read your hastily
written, weak, poorly thought-out first draft.
Then you made amends to them by giving
them a tight, well-reasoned manuscript that
had gone through no less than four rewrites.

**If You Want to Be a Knight,
You Have to Slay a Dragon** 70

STEP 9 | Made direct amends to those who've read 79
your inferior work wherever possible,
except when to do so would injure them or
others, especially you if you encounter them
in the future and they remember what terrible
tripe you wrote and will view you as a hack.

**How Much Time Can You Spend in Your Head,
Lost in Your Thoughts, Floating Aimlessly?** 80

STEP 10 | You continued to take personal inventory 87
and when you were wrong about not taking
constructive criticism and feedback you
promptly admitted it to those who took the
time to read your manuscript.

**The Best Part of Doing Cocaine
Is Going to Get It** 88

STEP 11 | You sought through prayer and meditation   97
to improve your conscious contact with
God, as you understood Him, praying only
for knowledge of His will for you and the
power to carry that out by changing your
disingenuous behavior and learning to get
some backbone when dealing with agents,
editors, managers, directors, and producers.

**When People Pleasers Stop Pleasing
People, People Aren't Pleased**   98

STEP 12 | Having had a spiritual awakening as the   105
result of these Steps, you tried to carry
this message to other blocked, stymied,
broken writers, and to practice these
principles in all your affairs.

**Hitting Bottom: Nothing Changes
If Nothing Changes**   106

**Epilogue For Comedy Writers, Who Live in Their
Own Special Hell**   111

A Special STEP 13 for Writers of Comedy   113
You admitted to God, to yourself, and to
fellow writers the exact nature of your
inability to understand how to write a
comedy, funny lines, comical situations,
and comedic characters.

Comedy Writer: Heal Thyself!   114

About the Author   129

How Writers Rehab Can Work Best for You

Writers Rehab is designed to be a comprehensive self-help book in the form of a 12-Step Program for writers dealing with emotional or psychological roadblocks with their writing.

You can use it as a source to deal with the numerous scenarios that face writers: being stifled creatively, running into brick walls, losing confidence, and experiencing writer's block to the point of depression and creative collapse.

There are ways to get back on track, starting with the number 12, which is of great importance to writers.

Joseph Campbell's 12 Stages of the Hero's Journey is the foundation of storytelling.

As exemplified by Christopher Vogler in his classic work, *The Writer's Journey: Mythic Structure for Writers*, the 12 Stages are laid out and clearly explained as they pertain to screenwriting. They are also applicable to novels, plays, and television scripts.

However, depending on the story you're telling, you may not need to utilize all 12 Stages. You only have to use the ones your plot needs to keep the dramatic tension going. It is, however, important to understand what each Stage means towards building your story.

Using screenplays as an example, if you were writing an epic adventure along the lines of *Raiders of the Lost Ark* or *Lord of the Rings* you would use all 12 Stages. But if your next script is an earnest drama like *Little Children* or *Marilyn and Me*, you might need only four or five of the Stages.

You would figure out which Stages would best serve the story you are telling.

Writers Rehab works much the same way in that there are 12 Steps, each dealing with a different aspect of the problems preventing all writers from writing, completing, and rewriting their manuscripts to be good enough to go out into the marketplace.

As with the 12 Stages of the Hero's Journey, when you read the 12 Steps in *Writers Rehab*, you may find that not all are applicable to your unique situation and personality.

For example, Step 11 is about the negative effects of being a people-pleasing writer.

Let's say you have a wise-ass cousin or brother-in-law who likes to bust your chops about your writing career, which he perceives as lackluster. Needless to say, he's the kind of insensitive jerk who's never had a creative idea in his life, has no idea how the writing process works, and has zero knowledge of what it means for a writer to be blocked, depressed, or feeling hopeless.

Depending on your personality, it's very easy in situations like that to make excuses, be defensive, or just let him mess with you until he gets bored.

Step 11 would be right up your alley.

But what if you are *not*, by nature, a people pleaser? You may feel that this Step won't necessarily be of value to you.

And you might be right — for the moment.

But as legendary acting teacher Stella Adler liked to say, "Life intrudes," which is a classier way of saying that shit happens.

Down the road you travel as a novelist, screenwriter, playwright, or television writer, you may find yourself in a situation where you must capitulate to the ideas of a director, agent, manager, development executive, editor, or producer who has the ability to get you a deal. If you don't agree to the changes, the deal is off.

And you want that deal!

You *need* that deal for the money, your pride, and to make your significant other proud of you (and to shove it in the face of that obnoxious cousin or brother-in-law).

Perhaps you won't know how to handle the confrontation. Step 11 will help you understand what to do, what not to do and most importantly, why you're even considering being a people pleaser in this situation.

Questioning the kind of projects you've been writing? Scratching your head as to why they're not generating interest? Step 8 is for you. Maybe you've been told by agents, editors, or producers that what you've written is well written, but lacks commercial appeal. If you're a screenwriter perhaps you've been told your screenplays are too "indie" or too European in style, i.e., strong on character, soft on plot. Maybe your novels and plays have been viewed as old-fashioned or not edgy enough.

If that's the case, Step 8 will motivate you to rethink your wheelhouse and appreciate the value of walking away from your comfort zone.

Does criticism and feedback rankle you? Got a bit of a superiority complex? Think that you know best?

Step 7 will give you a wake-up call and explain why you need to get your ego in check to prevent you from experiencing a major crash and burn.

Maybe you consider yourself a results-oriented person. You come from a work ethic with the understanding that if you spend a year working your butt off on a project, you should get some kind of response soon after it's done. Unfortunately, the film/television/theater/publishing industries are a delayed-gratification world.

If you've felt the sting of getting little, if any, response to your work, Step 2 will give you another way of looking at things.

As you go through each of the 12 Steps, just as you would go through each of the 12 Stages of the Hero's Journey, process everything and act on that which can help you.

But remember: as you move forward both in your regular life and your life as a writer, things are always in motion, always changing: sometimes for the better, sometimes for the worse.

Just as you create problems, obstacles, and complications for your characters, the future may hold setbacks, conflicts, and situations currently not in your frame of reference.

But if and when they come, you'll know where to look for help.

Introduction
Writers on the Verge

As a writing teacher, writing coach, and script consultant for nearly 20 years — and a writer myself — I've learned that there are three stages in the life of a writer:

1. Getting a project written
2. Getting a deal
3. Getting it produced or published

Writers both new and experienced don't have much control over whether what they write reaches its final audience, but they can control the first stage.

A writer can't get anything written if he's not writing. Not being able to write is at its core a mental problem. Non-productivity is its own form of addiction and obsessive-compulsive behavior. The easiest thing in the world for a writer to do is avoid writing.

But when a writer is so bogged down in her inability to push forward with a script, complete a first draft (let alone revisions and a polish), or even get started on a new idea, she's in deep trouble and she knows it.

Not only do writers arrive at a point where they're unable to write, they find themselves not wanting to. Welcome to avoidance. They become experts in finding ways to avoid returning to the battle zone.

And it *is* a battle zone.

Until a writer finishes the first draft, his battle with his script, play, or novel is like being in a destructive, co-dependent relationship.

I am not a psychiatrist, therapist, mental health counselor, psychologist, psycho-dramatist, or even a licensed social worker, but as you go through this book you may feel as if you're experiencing some form of psychoanalysis.

That's my intent.

Don't think of me as an armchair general who has never been on the battlefield, or a Monday-morning quarterback who never played the game, pontificating about how you should get off the ground, dust yourself off, and start writing. Everything I talk about in these pages I've either experienced personally or directly through the many, many writers I know. I've had to deal with my own levels of success, close calls, deals that fell through, projects that almost happened, pilots that didn't make it to the air, and the frustration and disappointment that comes with things not working out the way I'd hoped.

I've done a lot of handholding, listening, counseling, sympathizing, and advising, and dished out my share of tough love to writers of all ages and genres.

Having been in therapy (couples, individual, and group) with three different shrinks (two men, one woman), I've worked through most of my issues. I've also picked up the lingo and logic from my own therapists and much reading. And it doesn't hurt that I've been listening to Dr. Drew for 15 years. I've learned to think like a shrink in many areas.

Three of the most important words I learned are *cognitive-behavioral therapy*. If you don't know what that is, here's a basic definition: It involves challenging a person's beliefs about himself and also changing his behavior.

For example, if I'm the therapist and you're the client and you said, "I'm no good," I might respond with something like "How so? How do you know? What evidence do we have to the contrary?"

And it goes on from there.

As you move through these pages, while I may often sound like a shrink, I'd rather you think of me as someone sitting in the same 12-Step Support Group with you. And please don't think of me as the leader of the group.

I wrote *Writers Rehab* following the model of AA meetings.* The only people in attendance at AA meetings are alcoholics. However, understand this: Alcoholism is a disease. It is not curable, but it can be put into remission. Being a blocked writer is not a disease, it's more of a condition or disorder, and it too can be put into remission. But as with alcoholism, it's always lurking.

Writers Rehab was written for blocked writers of every kind who've come to a point where they're immobilized, desperate, depressed, and psychically damaged, so imagine that there are only writers such as yourself at this meeting. This is not about making it big as a writer, i.e., getting deals, making

---

*To emphasize my points, I have taken liberties with the official phrasing of The 12 Steps of Alcoholics Anonymous. The 12 Steps in *Writers Rehab* are intended to be read as if you are admitting to each of your weaknesses and relating what you have done to apologize to those whom you might have offended. Read aloud the steps of *Writers Rehab* the first time you encounter each of them to reinforce your commitment to achieving your goals and moving on.

money, and watching your creation get published or produced. It's about finding out why you're not writing and getting you back on track.

AA has no official counselors, social workers, or doctors. What's more, everyone is equal — there is no formal group leader. But for our purposes here, pretend that I'm a veteran at these meetings and you're here for the first time.

Welcome. My name is D.B. and I'm a writer who couldn't get his acts together.

D.B. Gilles
New York City

Who looks outside, dreams;
who looks inside, awakes.

CARL JUNG

STEP 1 | You admitted you were powerless over your inability to write and that your writing life had become unmanageable.

It's Time to Stop Bullshitting Yourself

There's an old saying in poker, that if you look around the card table and don't see a sucker, the sucker is you.

As a writer who's having problems writing, when you look for someone to blame, don't waste time bullshitting yourself: That person is you.

Not your agent or manager (if you're lucky enough to have one), not the producer(s), director(s) or theater artistic director(s) who have strung you along and broken your spirit for so long it's thrown you into a tailspin, not the teacher who doesn't think your script/short story/novel/play is up to par, not the contest judges who didn't declare you the winner, not your significant other who withheld support, not the members of your writing group who failed to offer the positive reactions you expected. Not anyone.

It's you!

The sooner you acknowledge that, the better off you'll be and the sooner you can get your act together. Much like the alcoholic or gambler or cokehead who must first admit that there is a problem, you do too.

You're the one avoiding your computer. You're the one killing time doing other stuff when you should be writing or taking a fresh look at the project that brought you to your knees, or finding the emotional strength to begin a new one.

Own that fact and maybe you can get out of the doldrums, assuming you *want* to. There's great comfort in feeling sorry for yourself. Whining, bitching, and moaning are great escapist tactics.

I hate being around complainers and whiners, not just writers, but in my real life. They drain me. They bore me. They anger me. They certainly don't inspire me. Who inspires me? Writers who write. Writers who get knocked down and get back up and keep going even if they've gone years without much success (or any success).

People like that are inspirational.

Maybe you like *not* writing. Maybe you do manage to finish a draft or even several drafts and then you fall apart when you try to get the script out there.

As the saying goes, "writers like having written." But you're not even doing that. I'm of the belief that you shouldn't be a writer unless you love writing.

If you don't love it, why bother? There's too much frustration and angst involved.

Maybe you wither like a snowflake at the first rejection.

Maybe you're much better at whining about how unfair the pursuit of a screenwriting career is.

You're right. It *is* unfair.

Tough shit. Deal with it or get out of the race. And it is a race. It's a marathon, not a sprint. How long can you last? How far can you go? How much are you willing to take?

Especially if you don't have your head screwed on straight.

Look, depression sucks. So does negative thinking. So does procrastination, fear, low self-esteem, losing your confidence, despair, hopelessness, and all the other moods, dispositions, and downbeat, harmful frames of mind that poison the psyche and crush your creativity.

It's hard to write when you're wrapped up in your

own lack of productivity, consumed by fear and lost in destructive thoughts.

Just as an alcoholic must first admit there is a problem, so must you. What you're going through is more than writer's block. You're avoiding writing. That may not be a disease according to *The New England Journal of Medicine*, but it is a serious condition and it's destroying you.

So go ahead. Admit to yourself that your mental state is getting in the way of your writing. Acknowledge that you may have deep-seated psychological reasons why you're not writing. Doing so doesn't mean you're mentally ill. Are alcoholics mentally ill? No. They have a disease and there are things they can do to curtail it.

You have a condition and there are things you can do to cure it.

If you've never been to therapy, it's time to start. Just as all works of fiction must start with instigating events or inciting incidents, so does most people's entrance into the world of therapy. Therapists like to call it the precipitating event, i.e., the thing in your life that you are unable to handle. The thing that all your previous coping mechanisms can no longer protect you from.

And even more importantly, don't ignore the fact that you may be clinically depressed.

Yes.

According to Daniel K. Hall-Flavin, M.D., depression ranges in seriousness from mild, temporary episodes of sadness to severe, persistent depression. Doctors use the term "clinical depression" to describe the more severe form of depression, also known as "major depression'" or "major depressive disorder."

Sound like anybody you know?

It's okay to admit it. You won't be the first and certainly won't be the last.

Clinical depression isn't the same as depression caused by a loss (such as the death of a loved one), substance abuse, or a medical condition such as a thyroid disorder.

Clinical depression symptoms usually improve with psychological counseling, antidepressant medications, or a combination of the two. Even severe depression symptoms usually improve with treatment.

Clinical depression symptoms may include:
- Depressed mood most of the day, nearly every day. *What a drag, right?*

- Loss of interest or pleasure in most activities. *Sound familiar?*
- Significant weight loss or gain. *Clothes been fitting a little snug lately? Or loose?*
- Sleeping too much or not being able to sleep nearly every day. *Could this be you?*
- Slowed thinking or movement that others can see or fatigue or low energy nearly every day. *Well?*
- Feelings of worthlessness or inappropriate guilt. *Been there, done that.*
- Loss of concentration or indecisiveness. *Oh yeah.*
- Recurring thoughts of death or suicide. *Sometimes. Not often, but sometimes.*

To meet the criteria for clinical depression you must have five or more of the above symptoms over a two-week period. At least one of the symptoms must be either a depressed mood or a loss of interest or pleasure.

Keep in mind, some types of depression may not fit this strict definition.

Thank you, Dr. Hall-Flavin.

Based on the hundreds of screenwriters, novelists,

comedy writers, playwrights and television writers who've shared their innermost thoughts and fears with me, I feel strongly that one or all of the above points have prevented numerous projects from being finished or rewritten to a stage where they're good enough to have a shot.

If any or all of the above is resonating with you, it's time to do something about it.

If you're currently unwilling or not ready to consider therapy, this book was written with the specific goal of helping you get there, if indeed you need to be there.

Exercise

Read Abraham Maslow's *Hierarchy of Needs* which you can Google. Beyond the details of air, water, food, and sex, he names five broader layers:

- Physiological
- Safety and security
- Love and belonging
- Esteem
- Self-actualization

After reading what Maslow wrote, make a list of your needs as a writer; specifically, what you expected to get from the profession, what you've gotten, what you haven't gotten, and what changes in your behavior you're prepared to make in order to achieve your goals.

Most people never run far enough on their first wind to find out they've got a second.

WILLIAM JAMES

STEP 2 | You came to believe that a Power greater than yourself could restore you to help you regain control of that plot that wouldn't bend.

We Want What We Want When We Want It

Writing is not a profession for anyone who's used to being paid after putting in a day's work. Punch in/ punch out. Do your 40 hours. Get a paycheck at the end of the week.

When you're a results-oriented person in the delayed-gratification world of film, television, publishing, and the theater, it brings you down.

Way down.

If you went to college, you put in your four years and you got a degree. Put in two or three more years for grad school and you get a degree. Put in however long it takes to write your dissertation and you're a Doctor.

You put in the effort and you get a reward. Makes sense.

What doesn't make sense is when you put in the effort and there's no reward. Let's talk about screenwriting. Writing a spec screenplay — whether you spend five weeks, eight months or two years — doesn't guarantee a reward.

For some, that's very upsetting, especially if you're a results-oriented person. Most of us are results oriented. Who wants to do anything without some remuneration? Even a college student who gets a job as an unpaid intern will have a payback down the road: experience, maybe a promotion to a paying job upon graduation, possibly a good reference. So there is a payback.

But if you take up screenwriting you must accept the fact that your results-oriented work ethic doesn't mean crap. You have entered a new world of delayed gratification. Put in the time — months, years, lots of sweat and energy — with the idea that there will be a payoff later on.

There might be.

There might not.

No matter how good or commercial your first screenplay is, it may never earn you a penny or get you an agent. Its only purpose may be to have helped you get your feet wet as a screenwriter. Same with your second, third, fourth, and fifth screenplays.

Lots of hard work, but no deals, agents, or managers. Maybe access to some producers, which is something.

But with each script, you're getting better. Most of us, myself included, after we've written a few screenplays, can look objectively at our first or second and realize that they were, at best, workmanlike. Maybe even pretty mediocre.

Same with your first few plays or novels.

Delayed gratification should be your mantra.

I will do the work and put in the time because I believe in myself and my talent. I understand that this is a marathon and it's not fair and that some people sell the first freakin' thing they write. I can no longer follow my results-oriented attitude and must accept the fact that I will hopefully taste the honey at some point. I know that the more I write the better I'll get and that has to be consolation enough until my pay day comes.

If you can't abide by this way of thinking, writing will be a troubling, frustrating, and, frankly, soul-crushing experience.

That's why you need to find a mentor. No matter how old you are.

And it can't be just anyone.

Whether it's in life or in the context of pursuing a career as a writer, the presence of a mentor is important. Nobody does it alone, without guidance, without someone to motivate you or push you or talk some sense into you. If you're lucky enough to have someone who cares enough to want to inspire you to do better or to overcome those demons that have immobilized you and are preventing you from completing the first draft of your screenplay or getting the energy to start that rewrite, you're a fortunate person.

But some of us don't have a mentor. Maybe we had one or two, but we were too arrogant or insecure to listen to them. Add to the mix the fact that you're no longer in high school or college and the odds of finding potential mentors become increasingly low, or you might be too egotistical to want to listen to anyone.

But I'm not here to judge. I want this to be a judgment-free environment.

Let's just say that you would like to have a mentor, but the pickings are slim.

What do you do?

Be your own mentor.

Learn how to inspire yourself, to push yourself, to

get focused and to face the harsh reality that your career is not moving forward (let alone your script, novel or play) and the only person to blame is you. (I know I said I want this to be a judgment-free environment, so don't think of those last seven words as judgment, but rather fact).

Just as you know when you've eaten too many Mallomars at one sitting or had too many margaritas or behaved irresponsibly in some situation, you also know when you're not writing. You know what it's like to turn your frustration outward, when you should be turning it inward. By looking at yourself in a critical way, if you have the guts, you'll pinpoint what's preventing you from writing at all or completing your project.

There's nothing like a little fire in the belly to jump-start a session at the computer. And there's nothing like some solid introspection and self-analysis to bring you to a moment of clarity.

It's real easy for all of us to BS our way into or out of anything, but that's negative behavior. No mentor worth his or her salt will ever BS you. Mentors tell the truth, whether we want to hear it or not. And, guess what, we don't want to hear it.

Compliments are nice, but it's the stuff we don't want to hear that will help us move forward.

If there's no mentor in your life presently and if you don't see anyone on the horizon, it's time to take charge and get the job done yourself.

Remember, no one will care as much about your writing and your writing career as you.

Exercise

As your own mentor, tell yourself to go back to the time when you first wanted to be a writer. Maybe you were 11 years old, in high school or college, or 30 or 50 and upwards.

Try to recall your exact state of mind. The enthusiasm and excitement you felt as you made the decision to take a shot at writing something.

Try to remember your first idea or ideas. If you still have your earliest outlines, notes, random musings, and early partial drafts, look at them and try to remember what was going on in your head back then.

Then create a timeline to the present and make a list of the false starts or shaky rough drafts and see if you can find a pattern of stopping and starting with large gaps in between.

If you find such a pattern, it's clearly your modus operandi and your objective is to change it.

If you're going through hell,
keep going.

WINSTON CHURCHILL

STEP 3 | You made a decision to turn your clichéd, underdeveloped protagonists and meandering subplots over to the care of God and a firm grasp of the 3-Act structure as you understood Him and it.

If You Want to Drown, Why Torture Yourself by Swimming in Shallow Water?

How much do you have to write before you throw in the towel? Three novels? Four screenplays? Six television pilots? Eight plays?

It depends on how seriously you take your writing career — even if you don't technically have a career.

Maybe all you've got are a few projects that have been rejected (if you're fortunate enough to have had them read by someone in the industry, even if they said no). And even worse, the only person who has read your work is unqualified to offer worthwhile feedback. Like your film-buff cousin who thinks *Citizen Kane* is overrated or your sister-in-law who quotes Harry Potter chapter and verse.

FYI, in the hierarchy of writing, having a project rejected means that you're at least *in* the game. Not having it read by even the youngest newbie working as an editorial assistant or development intern means you're spinning your wheels.

Getting that first rejection means you've drawn blood. Actually, your blood has been drawn. You're in the war! Well, game. No, *war* because with each project you have a new battle and you will shed new blood and tears. Maybe not literally blood, but don't rule out the tears.

If you want to be a writer, rejection goes with the territory — as if you've never heard that before. I'm just reminding you in case you're in denial or if you're new to this game (let's just call it a game, it's less ominous); I want you to learn the ropes quickly. For writers, at least for the hundreds of writers I've encountered over the last 20 years, rejection is hardwired into their souls.

Rejection followed by discouragement, followed by heartbreak, followed by despair.

By the way, this is not intended to make you feel good.

It's supposed to be a wake-up call and make you confront the possibility that it might be time to walk away from the writing game.

Once you've been getting your work read for two or three years (which means you've probably written at least one and maybe three or four things), here's what should be part of your DNA:

- Without an agent or manager, your chances are pretty slim of getting your manuscript read. So you've tried the "sending manuscripts to production companies and publishers" route.

- If you can't get anyone at a production company or publisher to read your work, you enter contests.

- If you don't win or place highly in contests, you go the paid-subscription approach where for a fee you receive notices of what producers are looking for.

- The Luck Factor. You're waiting to be lucky and by that I mean you're in the right place at the right time and you get a chance to pitch an idea *or* you meet someone who knows someone and will refer you.

I know a screenwriter who got a major agent because his girlfriend babysat for the agent's wife and she pressured the woman to read her boyfriend's script, and after reading it the wife gave it to her husband who liked it, then signed the screenwriter, who got a deal and has had a very nice career.

If you're at a different level career-wise, i.e., you *have* an agent or manager (or gone through more than one), your work is getting read, you're taking meetings, you're getting a little buzz, you maybe even had a deal and actually got some money and the project started moving forward and... then it fell apart (because of nothing *you* did)... then you're in a different kind of bad place than the writer who can't even get material read.

You're in that dark place where you're losing faith in the system. Maybe five years have gone by and despite all your efforts your "career" has stalled and despite all that you've learned, you haven't sold anything and it's getting to you.

Your once cheery optimism is beginning to crack and you're being increasingly skeptical. You joke that you now have a healthy cynicism. Now, instead of *expecting* to sell what you've written, you're more cautious and thinking it probably won't sell, but you're still keeping the faith.

Skip ahead five more years and (assuming you can write one per year) five more screenplays.

Still nothing, but you're closer; a different agent, classier production companies, better regional theaters, more respected publishers, a little money, but... no real money and nothing produced or in print. You still have your day job. If you're a screenwriter, maybe you've actually crashed through the void and gotten some decent cash and the movie was made which puts you in yet a different category: the screenwriter who had a screenplay made.

Skip ahead five more years and five more screenplays or plays or novels.

You know where this is going.

I know many writers who are enormously talented and have been fighting the good fight for many years. Some have had a smidgeon of success by winning a contest or having a quality producer option their script and take them through rewrites and get meetings and forward movement and rewrites and... well, still no movie in the can.

As I said earlier (and certainly others before me), pursuing a career as a writer no matter what your genre is a marathon race. In 1969 a film starring Jane Fonda opened called *They Shoot Horses, Don't They?* about marathon dancers during the Great Depression. Poor kids would compete in dance marathons for a cash prize. A catchphrase from the movie was "How long can they last?" Meaning, how long will the dancing kids last until they drop from exhaustion? Did I mention that they had to "dance" 24 hours a day? Only bathroom breaks. See the movie. It's amazing. (And needless to say, it probably wouldn't get made in the Hollywood of today because of its downer story and existential theme).

"How long can they last?" as it pertains to writers should read, "How long will *you* last?"

Only you know the answer. My feeling is that most writers who've been at it a long time without success will quit when they've had enough. That could be after only three screenplays. Others stay in it for the long haul hoping for the big break.

Maybe you should give up. But *don't* unless you have truly had it. The love is gone. The passion is gone. It's like a relationship that's become too painful to endure. It's time to get out.

But if it hasn't gotten to that point for you and you still have fire in your belly, consider the French proverb: "One may go a long way after one is tired."

And despite the passage of years and close calls and disillusioning phone calls from producers and agents and deals that almost happened — if you *still* enjoy writing, stay the course.

When you put it in the context of "it's the journey not the destination," isn't being a writer really all about the writing? There are many screenwriters who've had their screenplays made and butchered. *They're* less happy and as frustrated as you for entirely different reasons.

There's an old saying, "Don't be discouraged. It's often the last key in the bunch that opens the lock."

Keep writing. But if you've had it, quit now.

Exercise

Watch the 1988 film *Clean and Sober*, starring Michael Keaton and recounting his character's trouble with substance abuse. I'll reveal no more of the plot so as not to spoil things, but watch it not only because it's a great film, but because it takes you into the world of someone who, by being consumed by his addiction, has lost sight of reality. It's also a flawlessly structured screenplay. Pay close attention to the end of Act One and end of Act Two events that propel the story forward.

If you've never been in therapy (and even if you have) watch the HBO series *In Treatment*.

The reason to take a serious look at these works is because it may introduce you to a world that you know nothing about or you have denied you need to know more about.

If the shoe fits... you know the drill.

*You must do the things
you think you cannot do.*

ELEANOR ROOSEVELT

STEP 4 | You made a searching and fearless moral inventory of the troublesome 256-page romantic subplot you thought would add a magical realism to your bloated 981-page first draft that didn't get started until page 189.

Scared Money Never Wins

Maybe it's time to get out of your comfort zone and change your wheelhouse. Maybe you're afraid. I don't blame you. You should be.

The title of this chapter is another cool poker adage: If you're afraid to take a risk, you're never gonna win. That's a fairly tame piece of reality. Lotto commercials have been saying for years that "you've gotta be in it to win it."

The "reality" of pursuing a career as a writer is such that it defies any kind of logic. Vladimir Nabokov says that "reality is the one word that is meaningless without quotation marks." Being a writer is an endeavor that takes armadillo-thick skin and monumental courage, not just now, but ever since magazines began publishing short stories, theaters began producing plays, publishers began putting out books and Hollywood started making movies.

As I'll discuss in greater detail in Step 6, you are in many ways the protagonist in your own movie as a writer. You must embark on the 12 Stages of the Hero's Journey as explained by Joseph Campbell and expanded upon in writings by Christopher Vogler, as mentioned earlier in How Writers Rehab Can Work Best for You.

Most of the writers I encounter, be they newbies or people starting their tenth script, are wondering if there's a particular road to take that will lead to selling their work.

There isn't.

It's different for everyone. Some sell the first thing they write, others keep moving along inch by inch, script by script, year by year without getting a break.

Years ago I heard a Hollywood maxim stated by the actor Cliff Robertson: "The greatest talent is the ability to recognize talent." I think that means that an agent, manager, editor, producer, actor, or someone with clout has the ability to read a novel or screenplay, recognize its quality (as well as its flaws), have a gut feeling as to its commercial potential, know how to guide the writer into making it even better (maybe even "great"), thus more saleable, and then running with it to try and make the project happen.

If you're lucky you'll find someone like that.

If not, maybe it's time to rethink your approach to creativity, i.e., finding ideas.

Forget about writing a good script. Forget about writing a "great script." What you need to focus on is writing something that someone important, with access to people who can make things happen, thinks he or she can sell.

I have read many excellent screenplays and a few "great" ones, but for a variety of reasons, they never sold:

- The subject matter wasn't commercial.
- The story was too downbeat.
- Not enough appeal to a mass audience.
- Not enough appeal to the 12-24 audience.
- Not enough appeal to get entire families in theaters, including grandparents.
- Too expensive.
- The lead character is too old.
- The lead character isn't likable.
- The lead character isn't sympathetic.
- The ending isn't happy enough.
- The lead character isn't big enough to interest a star.

- An agent or manager tells you, "I can't sell it in this market."
- You find out somebody else has written the exact same story and has not only sold the script, but it's in production. You'd be surprised how often this happens. Maybe it's happened to you. It happened to me twice. Once with a screenplay, another time with a play.
- It's not high concept enough.

There are probably more reasons fine screenplays don't sell (or get made) that I haven't listed. If you're a screenwriter you may have your own unique anecdote.

But is there really a way to have a better shot at selling your work?

Maybe.

If you write stories inspired by your personal experiences (that weird camping trip you took last summer, the eccentric girl you dated who was a stripper by night and a PhD candidate in nuclear physics by day, the all-gay high school basketball team your brother played on), you may have more of a problem than someone who makes stuff up. Your creativity relies on stuff you draw from your experience.

That's fine, but I believe a writer is in a better, stronger place if she has a vivid imagination.

So if you're the kind of writer who uses that imagination to write material that would be considered a tough sell, maybe the time has come to put on that high-concept thinking cap.

What's high concept? The best definition I've ever heard was from screenwriter Dale Launer (*My Cousin Vinny*, *Dirty Rotten Scoundrels*, etc.) and it's basically that when someone tells you the premise of their script you smile.

Works for me.

Now that doesn't mean that if you tell someone what your idea is about and he doesn't smile it's a bad idea. It's just not a particularly commercial idea.

Case in point. *My Big Fat Greek Wedding* (2002) written by Nia Vardalos. This was a monster hit! An amazing romantic comedy.

The premise, as it appears on IMDb.com:
A young Greek woman falls in love with a non-Greek and struggles to get her family to accept him while she comes to terms with her heritage and cultural identity.

If Nia Vardalos had told you the premise you probably wouldn't have smiled. Neither would I. That plot is not high concept. It sounds kind of old fashioned.

But the execution of that ordinary idea certainly made lots of people smile, including me.

Look at 2009's *(500) Days of Summer* written by Scott Neustadter and Michael H. Weber.

Again, from IMDb.com:
An offbeat romantic comedy about a woman who doesn't believe true love exists, and the young man who falls for her.

Uh, well, okay.

Pretty soft.

Not to mention pretty vague.

I would not have smiled if the authors pitched it to me and I'd bet you wouldn't have either, but the execution of the screenplay was wonderful!

The other side of this coin is that just because you have a high-concept idea that makes everyone you tell it to giggle like idiots doesn't mean they'll be smiling if the execution sucks.

Ah, that word "execution." It is the bane of every writer's existence.

Take *Little Nicky* (2000) starring Adam Sandler. Here's the IMDb.com Logline:
A movie about the independent minded son of Beelzebub and the mischief he creates.

The IMDb.com Logline doesn't do it justice. A better description would be that Adam Sandler plays the son of the devil and that his mother is an angel so he has a hard time being bad because he's a hybrid.

That's a decent high-concept premise, but the execution of the script didn't serve the idea well. I actually had an opportunity to read the screenplay and was not impressed. The movie, which I also saw, tanked and was one of Sandler's few bombs.

So, bottom line, I'm suggesting that if by nature you don't come up with high-concept ideas, give it a shot. You have nothing to lose. Let your mind wander. Check the tabloids for bizarre/wacky/silly events that with the right spin could become a screenplay. And if you get your ideas from what you've personally experienced, look for the off-the-hook event in your life that was so weird it just might make a good story.

Not that it'll be easy. It's just as difficult to find an amazing high-concept idea as it is to generate a great thriller, romantic comedy, or action story.

I've tried. My background is as a playwright, a dramatist if you will. When I got into screenwriting I stuck with the more dramatic stuff, then gradually came up with ideas that had a little more commercial potential, then out of sheer desperation I came up with a few high-concept ideas and guess what? I got three deals and another one optioned.

They weren't crazy/stupid/moronic high-concept ideas like so many that actually get produced. They accomplished what a good high concept is supposed to: everyone I pitched it to smiled.

If there's a new approach that you haven't tried in order to make a sale, take your shot at something high concept. It's no "easier" finding those ideas than anything else you've come up with, but when you're fortunate enough to find one, if you can pull off the execution you just might find yourself swimming in different waters.

Exercise

The more writers you're exposed to, the better.

If you're a screenwriter or thinking of writing a screenplay, below is the Web address to audio interviews with many screenwriters who talk about their experiences in Hollywood.

The website is screenwritersutopia.com and here's the address: http://www.screenwritersutopia.com/interviews/

As you hear these screenwriters talk about their careers and experiences, you'll see how each found his own unique road to selling that first script. Before that happened they were just like you, filled with hope, doubt, frustration, and dreams.

Ever tried? Ever failed?
No matter. Try again.
Fail again. Fail better.

SAMUEL BECKETT

STEP 5 | Admitted to God, to yourself, and to another human being the exact nature of your inability to stick to a project once you've begun without throwing in the towel and starting something new only to give up on that one too.

Don't Be an 80-Percenter

Finish: to bring a task or activity to an end; complete.

Better to fail big and write something shitty that you've at least finished, even if it came in too short or went way too long. Even if you're not sure who the main character is. Even if you're not entirely clear as to what the story is. Even if you find it impossible to pinpoint the genre.

You may decide not even to show it to anyone because you know it's so horrible, but at least you stayed the course and finished it.

You gave 100 percent to finishing a project and you failed. So what if it sucked and you deleted it from your computer and burned the only hard copy you made.

You didn't give up.

That's the first step toward not being an 80-percenter. That's someone who makes a partial, incomplete effort. They only give an 80-percent effort.

What's the next step?

Learning to push yourself through that remaining 20 percent. You've heard the maxim, "A quitter never wins and a winner never quits."

That's even more true when it applies to the ferocity in which you pursue your writing career. You can't be lazy. You can't half-ass it. You can't *sort of* be a writer.

Don't Be a Perfectionist with Your First Draft

By definition, perfectionism is the refusal to accept any standard short of perfection. This to me is an incredibly lofty goal. It's also fraught with the potential of tension and anxiety whether it's a kid in fifth grade who desperately stresses himself out in the pursuit of an A, a young parent trying to be Super Mom by multi-tasking until she's ready to drop, or a guy whose perfectionism is largely based on fear: fear of being judged, embarrassed, not good enough, et al.

But when it comes to writing, perfectionism at the first draft stage can be paralyzing. You can *perfect* your first draft into obscurity. Like rewriting the first chapter of your novel or the first 15 pages of your screenplay over and over again instead of plowing through to the end.

Perfectionism is another form of paralysis. In writing, as in life, perfectionism can paralyze or keep you running in place.

Forget Your Parents' Expectations That Have Haunted You Since Childhood

The Drama of the Gifted Child by Alice Miller should be read by every adult writer who had demanding parents. Miller's main point in the book is that the gifted child — the child who is more intelligent, more sensitive, and more emotionally aware than other children — can be so attuned to her parents' expectations that she does whatever it takes to fulfill these expectations while ignoring her own feelings and needs. In becoming the "perfect" child of her parents' dreams, the gifted child loses something very precious. She loses her true self. In becoming her parents' ideal child, she locks away her true feelings in a kind of "glass cellar," the key to which is thrown away.

Worry About Doing a Good First Draft Instead of a Perfect One

Grind out those first 350-500 pages if it's a novel, 90-120 pages if it's a screenplay, 80-100 pages if it's a play. No matter how long or short it is, just finish it. The longest screenplay I ever read was 238 pages. And it was good. The author didn't realize that he'd actually written a mini-series. It could've also served as an outline for an hour-long 12-episode TV drama.

Don't worry about chapters or scenes that are too short or too long or too talkie or overly described. Just get the fucking thing down on paper. Then, with each subsequent draft, continue to make it better and better and better. But not perfect. That will take forever.

B.F. Skinner says, "A failure is not always a mistake, it may simply be the best one can do under the circumstances. The real mistake is to stop trying."

Exercise

Read *Bird by Bird* by Anne Lamott, and the first thing to read is the section on *Shitty First Drafts*. Savor every word of this fantastic book.

*Creativity requires
the courage to let go
of certainties.*

ERICH FROMM

STEP 6 | You're entirely ready to have God help you create complex characters who resemble three-dimensional human beings rather than trite, shallow, stick figure characters we've seen a million times before.

Disappointment and Anxiety Are Messengers Saying You Are Headed for Unknown Territory

Put aside the fictional characters you create. The character you need to work on most is yourself.

The unknown territory referred to above is the part of your psyche that you have either never known existed or intentionally avoided.

Don't feel too bad. Most people intentionally avoid anything that might cause pain.

How analytical and psychological are you? Do you avoid thinking about unpleasant truths about yourself? Your parents? Your upbringing? Your marriage? Your children? The bad choices you've made? Do you have the capacity to acknowledge difficult truths about aspects of your life?

Are you able to look at yourself and see not only the good points, but also the bad? Or even your dark side? Politicians are often said to have public, private, and secret lives.

I believe we all do, even the kindest, most religious, and spiritual among us.

If you can look at yourself and, more importantly, inside yourself, these words will be easier for you to take in. If you can't, in the words of Margo Channing as portrayed by Bette Davis in *All About Eve* (written by Joseph L. Mankiewicz), "Fasten your seatbelts. It's going to be a bumpy night."

. . . .

There comes a point where, as a creative person, you should welcome the unhappy, unpleasant, and unraveling events of your life. We don't learn that much from good experiences. It's the bad times that really teach us valuable life lessons. I tell my students that we can learn much more from watching bad movies or reading bad novels than good ones.

The goal of the writer is to create compelling, memorable characters. To see his protagonist become a lasting cultural icon: What greater tribute could a writer ask for? Think of a film character that you admire. Remember, some writer somewhere made up that character. You should strive to create iconic personae as well.

Consider all the unforgettable characters that have entertained audiences over the years. Here are a few of mine:

- Macbeth
- Annie Hall
- Tony Soprano
- Blanche Dubois
- Sherlock Holmes
- Scarlett O'Hara
- Rocky Balboa
- Ebenezer Scrooge
- Dirty Harry
- Hawkeye Pierce
- Willy Loman
- Holden Caulfield
- Luke Skywalker
- Harry Potter
- Dracula
- Lisbeth Salander
- Archie Bunker
- James Bond

But before you can conjure up a remarkable character, you should consider reevaluating the most important character in your life:

You.

Not your significant other, not your kids, not your family. You're no good to anyone else if you're a mess.

Disappointment in all areas is, well, disappointing. We're disappointed when we can't make a story work. We're disappointed when we manage to finish a first draft and we hate what we've done. We're disappointed with the feedback we get on a project we're convinced is great. We're disappointed when we can't get an agent or editor or producer who likes it, let alone loves it. We're disappointed when we find out — after we finish the final rewrite and we're ready to start submitting it to people and places — that another script, similar to ours, has just gone into production.

Disappointment leads to anxiety.

What exactly is anxiety?

Simple definition:
A feeling of worry, nervousness, or unease, typically

about an imminent event or something with an uncertain outcome.

Broader definition:
Anxiety is a general term for several disorders that cause nervousness, fear, apprehension, and worrying. These disorders affect how we feel and behave, and they can manifest real physical symptoms. Mild anxiety is vague and unsettling, while severe anxiety can be extremely debilitating, having a serious impact on our daily lives.

People often experience a general state of worry or fear before confronting something challenging such as a test, examination, recital, or interview. In our case, it's writing, completing, and selling something we've written, or dealing with individuals whom we need to help us sell it. These feelings are easily justified and considered normal. Anxiety is considered a problem when symptoms interfere with a person's ability to sleep or otherwise function. Generally speaking, anxiety occurs when a reaction is out of proportion with what might be normally expected in a situation.

Any of this ringing a bell?

When I tried to leave my playwriting and screen-writing wheelhouse I started writing a novel. In retrospect, it took me much longer than it should have to complete.

Why? Because I was filled with incredible anxiety and self-doubt. I was used to writing half-hour sitcom scripts that were 30 to 35 pages, plays that were anywhere from 80 to 100 pages, and screenplays that came in around 110 pages.

Novels were supposed to be between 75,000 and 80,000 words, which is roughly 350 double-spaced pages. The sheer length of a novel terrified me. Writing a novel made all the other things I'd written seem like a day at the beach.

I'd start and stop, again and again. Sometimes for a year or two, then go back to it, get enthused only to walk away from it yet again.

I didn't understand it at the time, but I was consumed with anxiety that was exacerbated by my fear of not completing it.

Methods for treating anxiety include cognitive-behavioral therapy, psychotherapy, psychological counseling, medications, or a combination of therapies.

Ultimately, the treatment path depends on the cause of the anxiety and the patient's preferences.

Sometimes alcoholism, depression, or other co-existing conditions have such a strong effect on a person that treating the anxiety disorder must wait until the coexisting conditions are brought under control.

Cognitive-behavioral therapy attempts to recognize and change the patient's thinking patterns that are associated with the anxiety and wearisome feelings. This type of therapy has two main parts: a cognitive part designed to limit distorted thinking and a behavioral part designed to change the way people react to the objects or situations that trigger anxiety.

For example, a patient undergoing cognitive-behavioral therapy for panic disorder might work on learning that panic attacks are not really heart attacks. Those receiving this treatment for obsessive-compulsive disorder for cleanliness may work with a therapist to get their hands dirty and wait increasingly longer amounts of time before washing them.

And, of course, psychotherapy means working with a psychiatrist or psychologist. Similar forms of talk therapy can be conducted by trained mental health professionals, social workers, and other counselors.

Sessions may be used to explore the causes of anxiety and possible ways to cope with symptoms.

Is this making you uncomfortable?

Ringing any additional bells?

Is the thought of going to a therapist scaring the hell out of you? Disgusting you because you think only weak people see shrinks? Making you feel like a loser or stupid or crazy?

Join the club.

Most people who finally decide to go to therapy resist it at first.

I did.

For 20 years.

And I went in with great resistance and reluctance.

If you're resisting, there's always drugs. Not the fun kind, but rather prescriptive such as antidepressants, benzodiazepines, tricyclics, and beta-blockers. These are used to control some of the physical and mental symptoms.

I'll say it: You probably need help. You need to talk to someone other than your spouse, significant other, best friend, priest, rabbi, father, mother, or whoever it is that you'd normally go to when you feel that you're losing it and unable to cope.

It's your call.

Exercise

Write a character description of yourself, good points and bad. Think of yourself as the protagonist of your next novel, play or screenplay and you're creating a back story, but you're basing the character on yourself. Think of this as a test of your ability to be honest about your dark side.

Once you've completed the character description of yourself, start writing again or start thinking about gearing yourself up to start writing again.

If you are able to start writing, take small steps. Write for five minutes, then take a break. Or don't. Try writing for ten minutes, then take a break or stop for the day. Pat yourself on the back for getting started. If you write one page in those five minutes that's a victory. Give yourself credit for the small steps and the small victories.

There are several exercises, forms of meditation, and relaxation techniques that experts recommend to cope with this type of anxiety, which are beyond the scope of this book. Further information is readily available in bookstores or health food shops, or on the Internet.

Learn to replace "negative self talk" with "coping self talk." Make a list of the negative thoughts you have, and write a list of positive, believable thoughts to replace them.

There's always counseling and if you're not ready for that, consider seeking out a writers support group. Don't rule out starting one yourself.

Make your ego porous.
Will is of little importance,
complaining is nothing,
fame is nothing. Openness,
patience, receptivity,
solitude is everything.

RAINER MARIA RILKE

STEP 7 | Humbly asked God to remove your shortcomings, especially with regard to your inability to take criticism, to lose your ego, and to confront the deep-seated problems of what you've written.

Lose the Attitude, Ego & Superiority Complex

Did it ever occur to you that maybe you're not as talented a writer as you think? Is it possible you're not all that great, that you're only pretty good or okay or mediocre? And at the very worst, maybe you just don't have the goods.

There's nothing worse than a writer who thinks he knows best except, possibly, a writer who is delusional about his so-called talent.

Delusion: A belief that is not based in reality.

One of the most common is delusions of grandeur. People suffering from this believe they are special and more important than others. While one person's importance can be greater than others in certain situations, e.g., the President of the United States (or a movie star, a great athlete, or a famous author) shows up at an event, in 99 percent of other situations, the people are of equivalent status.

Delusions of grandeur cause the person to think he is more important than others, even when there is no particular reason or objective evidence for it. Sometimes, the delusional person believes he is a famous person or that he has a special relationship with a famous person.

How does this apply to writers?

Grandiosity can be an effect of some psychoactive drugs, most notably cocaine and crystal meth. This crosses over into delusion if the person is unable to see himself objectively and develops an exaggerated sense of his importance or self-worth. Sometimes, the delusion is in stark contrast with the reality of the way the person is perceived by others. However, some people don't need drugs to be grandiose. Their own insecurity is sufficient to exaggerate their importance to others.

In other words, a person might be perceived by everyone he knows as the biggest asshole in the world, a total fool, jerk or no-talent hack, but he isn't aware of it.

That's why self-awareness is so crucial to your mental well being, not to mention self-image. It's good to have an understanding of who you are — even if it means accepting the fact that you're a mediocre writer whose output needs lots of work.

. . . .

Writing teachers talk about character arcs and how a protagonist should change in the course of a film. The same thinking applies to everyone who's not being realistic and truthful about their talent.

I've encountered numerous arrogant writers who won't change a word, rewrite a scene, rethink a storyline, reexamine a character's motivations or listen to any other form of feedback. They take criticism personally. Their feelings are hurt.

Good!

Heartbreak, disappointment, and rejection should give you humility, in life and in your writing.

If you're one of those writers who cannot handle criticism, I feel sorry for you. You will not grow. You will wallow in your own dysfunction and, by the way, such behavior is indeed dysfunctional.

If the feedback you get isn't what you want to hear, you can react in two ways: listen to it or be defensive about it. It's that defensiveness that will bring you down. It's also the mark of an amateur. The professional welcomes feedback and opinions. The amateur is convinced he's right. The professional respects the value of listening. Maybe not everything that he hears he will agree with, but there will be certain comments he *will* agree with.

It's those comments that the professional will take in and process to make his manuscript better.

If you have a difficult time receiving negative feedback, you'd better get over it.

This is your livelihood. At least you want it to become your livelihood. So when something you've written — be it a line, monologue, scene, chapter, act, or entire script — isn't getting the response you hoped for, it means that what you've written needs to be examined. It means that it's just not good enough.

Don't be like the celebrity, professional athlete, or hotshot entrepreneur who surrounds himself with Yes men. Surround yourself with No men: with people, or at least one person, who will tell you the truth about your ho-hum novel, your ugly new sport coat, or the cheap yellow shoes you think make you look so hip.

Stop listening to anyone who enables you to ignore criticism of your writing.

Every so often on the news there's a story about some 500-pound guy who's so obese he has to be removed from his house by a crane in order to finally seek help at a hospital.

The guy can barely move and is unable to get out of bed. Someone is giving him food and lots of it. Someone is enabling him.

Give up all bad qualities in you, banish the ego, and develop the spirit of surrender. You will then experience bliss.

A little bliss would be nice, right? I bet that 500-pound guy would like some bliss.

Without getting your ego and overdeveloped sense of self in check, you might as well be that 500-pound guy in the form of a writer. The only difference is that we know who your enabler is: *you*!

Once you stop enabling yourself, start working on the humility thing and be open to the opinions of others who only want to make you a better writer; then you can open the door to the next stage of your career.

And maybe, just maybe, you'll even become a better person.

Exercise

Make a list of the people in your immediate circle of family, friends, and co-workers who you think you're smarter than. What are the shortcomings and limitations that make them a lower life form than you?

Then make a list of the people you know who you think are smarter than you. What are the strengths and attributes that you see in them that make them superior to your oversized ego?

Now make a list of the people in your life that you respect. People you know will always be truthful with you. People who won't coddle you. These may be people around whom you act like a different person. If you admire and respect your great-grand-father you might not show your true self to him. If there is such a person, ask yourself why you behave differently in front of him or her.

Look at all these names you've listed and find the one person you trust, above all others, and contact that individual. Tell him or her that you are trying to change your egotistical behavior and that you would like their help.

If you approach them with sincerity and truthfulness and your hat in your hand, with a little luck they'll reach out to you.

If not, find a therapist.

How to find one? Ask someone you know. If you're too embarrassed to do that, check your health provider. There are tons of therapists available.

Out of clutter, find simplicity.
From discord, find harmony.
In the middle of difficulty
lies opportunity.

ALBERT EINSTEIN

STEP 8 | You listed all the people you had harmed by asking them to read your hastily written, weak, poorly thought-out first draft. Then you made amends to them by giving them a tight, well-reasoned manuscript that had gone through no less than four rewrites.

If You Want to Be a Knight, You Have to Slay a Dragon

It's The Middle Ages. You're ambitious. You're not content to be a vassal or farmer or blacksmith or whatever your father and grandfather before you did for a living.

You want to be a knight. Knights were the rock stars of the time. They had the cool uniforms, the best horses, and probably got the hottest maidens.

Generally there were two ways that a boy could become a knight. The first was to be born into it. If a boy was the son of a knight or royalty he could be assured the opportunity of becoming a knight. At the age of eight, he would work for another knight as a page and have to learn all sorts of skills; then, if he were any good, in a few years he would become a squire. Then after more training and learning and grunt work, at the age of 20 he would become a knight.

That was the easy way.

For the guy without family connections it was tougher. He had to prove himself through bravery and prowess on the battlefield.

Let's say that the fastest track to knighthood was by slaying a dragon. If you did that, you could eliminate all the years of training and lots of battles.

Kings and queens loved knights who killed dragons. (I don't know that for sure, but if I were a king in sixteenth century France, I would sure as hell want a guy who killed a dragon to be on my payroll.)

Okay. Here's the shot: In today's competitive market, if you want to get a book or movie deal you'll have a better chance if your idea is highly commercial.

Yes, I'm talking about this again because it bears repeating.

Doesn't matter what the genre is, but if your Logline rocks and your Synopsis makes an agent, manager, editor, or producer drool because it's so cool and if the finished product lives up to their expectations and they see it as a star-driven vehicle (especially for a star they have access to) and if the screenplay or manuscript reads like a dream and if it has franchise potential and if they happen to know that a hotshot director is looking for something like what you wrote, well... you have slain the dragon!

If you're the kind of writer who writes non-commercial, thoughtful, "small" stories about real people in touchy-feely situations and if you don't think about making the big score, don't panic. It means you didn't want to be a knight anyway.

But if you're like that sixteenth century guy without connections who wants to be a knight, then you have to slay a dragon by writing a killer script.

Say you have a great idea? What good is it if you can't finish it?

Ordinary, workmanlike ideas are a dime a dozen.

Great ideas aren't. When I say great, I mean commercial, high concept, extremely sellable ideas. If you haven't figured it out yet, most of the time publishers, agents, and producers buy the "idea." It could be a book, play, comic strip, comic book, graphic novel, screenplay, blog, a true story and even a tweet.

If you're lucky enough to come up with a great idea, you move to the front of the line. But if you can't complete it, you're screwed. You're more screwed than the writer with an okay idea who has completed a script. At least he or she has something to put on the market. And sometimes that okay idea is so well executed that the writing stands out and the characters are so interesting that the okay idea is overlooked because reading it has been such an enjoyable ride.

Think *Juno* from 2007 written by Diablo Cody. Another really old, done-to-death idea:
Teenage girl gets pregnant, wants the right couple to adopt her child: Will she find the right couple?

Ho-hum.

But the execution, as we all know, was spot on. We hadn't heard dialogue like that in a while or seen such an appealing character. Hell, all the characters were appealing in this otherwise ordinary story.

So having the okay idea isn't necessarily a bad thing if you can rise to the occasion with superior execution.

But if you're one of those people with the "big" idea that would make even the most jaded Hollywood type or publisher do an Irish jig and you can't finish it, that's just bad form.

I can't tell you the number of great ideas I've heard from students, clients, friends, and colleagues. I mean, really cool things. The kind of idea you're immediately jealous of because you didn't think of it. The kind of idea that makes you want to suggest a collaboration.

And I can't tell you the number of great ideas I've heard that never get finished. Or maybe there's a first draft, but the author can't get the initiative to do the next couple of drafts to get it into the best possible shape.

Completion is everything. It's the only thing that matters if you want to have a career.

If you're one of those lucky people with a great idea, but you're not taking it to completion, you need to get in touch with why that's happening. Life intrudes, so if life is piling on and you can't get your head on straight, okay. But that doesn't mean you can't try to lift the fog.

Or maybe you need help in the form of a collaborator. You need a second set of eyes to help you discover what was right before your eyes. Maybe you need a script consultant or writing class or a writers support group.

It's bad enough to have an okay idea and not be able to complete it. But when you have that killer premise that makes everyone who you tell it to smile (and salivate with envy), and you can't get it done, it's not quite tragic, but it's pretty damn sad because the risk you take is that someone else will come up with the same idea and beat you to the punch.

Just wait for the idea to come, right?

Wrong!

Ideas, like opportunities, don't come that often. We have to look for them. Sometimes, if we're lucky, an idea for a screenplay appears out of nowhere. We're walking our dog, taking a shower, overhearing a conversation in a restaurant or an elevator, skimming the newspaper and voila!... inspiration strikes.

That's cool if that happens, but if we're spending the bulk of our time waiting for that fantastic idea to land in our laps, well, we're going to wait a long time. If the muse isn't striking a chord, we have to look for ideas. How do we do this? Pretty much by making sure our antennae are up 24/7.

Be on the lookout for ideas from all the different kinds of media. Read newspapers. Scope out all the pop culture Web sites. Check out the more out-rageous blogs. Listen to podcasts, see what's on Facebook, Tumbler, Twitter, and all social network-ing sites here now or to come.

When you're talking with friends or co-workers or strangers, pay attention to what they say. They might innocently relate an anecdote that resonates with you and could serve as the catalyst for your next writing project.

Let your mind wander. Think about your past: people, events, specific incidents that affected you. Some-times recalling things from our past opens up a door that has long been closed.

And don't forget about reading. Read novels. See plays (or read them). Or go to movies. Sometimes watching a film can jump-start your creativity. Inspi-ration breeds inspiration.

But the most important thing is to always be recep-tive to the random comment, encounter, or oddball incident that gets you to think, "What if...?"

Exercise

Make a list of the 10 most commercial movies and bestselling novels from the last 10 years. The genre doesn't matter. These are films and books that made a ton of money because they were very high concept.

Then write out the premise of each in a single sentence.

Then re-watch each film (or better yet, read the screenplay) and break down the structure into three acts. And reread the novels. Study the flow of dramatic tension, the pacing, the way characters are introduced.

And remember that you're reading the final draft or the shooting script and that their authors went through the same kind of hell you do when you're trying to complete, revise, refine, and sell a manuscript.

Neurotics complain of their illness,
but they make the most of it,
and when it comes to talking it
away from them they will defend it
like a lioness her young.

SIGMUND FREUD

STEP 9 | Made direct amends to those who've read your inferior work wherever possible, except when to do so would injure them or others, especially you if you encounter them in the future and they remember what terrible tripe you wrote and will view you as a hack.

How Much Time Can You Spend in Your Head, Lost in Your Thoughts, Floating Aimlessly?

There's an ironic saying among New York–based actors that, upon hearing it, you laugh, but upon thinking about it, you shake your head in frustration, and if you're living it, you cry:

> Guy #1
>
> Are you an actor?
>
> Guy #2
>
> I was until I moved to New York.

The actors from all over the country who have been acting in plays all their lives starting with elementary school, middle school, high school, community theater, college, summer stock, on cruises or wherever, arrive in New York with a solid résumé of credits only to stop getting parts.

The acting roles they were so accustomed to landing now come rarely or not at all. They audition and audition and audition but don't get cast. If they're lucky, maybe they get a small part or a few lines. And I'm not talking Broadway or even Off Broadway shows. I mean Off-Off Broadway plays, movies ranging from feature films (where they might be cast as an extra or as background) to low-budget independent films, or student films. Or they might find work in the handful of TV shows that shoot in New York who may need extras.

Even though they've been acting for years, they take acting classes, voice lessons, dance, you name it. They keep trying. Of course, some give up, leave the profession they dreamed of and find new careers, or they return to their hometowns and act in community theater.

In my opinion, if it was ultimately all about acting, they're better off. If it was about becoming a star, it's a different story.

The point of my talking about the plight of actors is this: If you want to be a writer to make big bucks and have your novels published or plays and films produced, fine; but if those are the only reasons, you will suffer. The larger reason you should want to be a writer is because you enjoy, or dare I say, *love* writing.

If at the end of your life you've written 37 screenplays, 14 plays, 11 television pilots, and 4 novels and nothing happened to any of them, so what? You experienced the creative satisfaction of writing them.

If it's all about the money, you'll experience emptiness. But, unlike the actors who leave New York or Los Angeles and spend their lives acting in community theater rather than pursuing the big dream, as a writer, you can keep going. You can continue to write, living where you live, working at however you make a living without giving up.

That's a blessing.

But only if you act on it.

You must take some dramatic action. You want the characters you create to move forward in their quest for whatever they want to happen, so why shouldn't you?

Inaction sucks!

Boat without a rudder, ship without a sail. You know what I mean.

Inaction breeds doubt and fear. Action breeds confidence and courage. The only way to conquer fear as a writer is to do something about it and the thing you must do is start writing. But before you can do that you need to figure out why you haven't been writing.

How hard is that? Not hard if you're honest with yourself.

That's what's hard. As I've stated before, we can all bullshit our way into, or out of, anything. I submit that there are no better people who are more crafty at kidding themselves than writers, be they screenwriters, novelists, playwrights, television writers, and even poets, probably.

If we're not writing, it's because we're finding ways to avoid it. We're using more energy and creativity to postpone a writing session than to sit down and force ourselves to do it.

Action is a great restorer and builder of confidence. Hopefully, the action you take will be successful and possibly different actions or adjustments will have to follow.

But any action is better than no action at all.

Creative risk-taking is essential for success in any endeavor where the stakes are high. Thoughtless risks are destructive, but perhaps even more wasteful is thoughtless caution, which prompts inaction and promotes our failure to seize opportunity.

Churchill said, "Want of foresight, unwillingness to act when action would be simple and effective, lack of clear thinking, confusion of counsel until the emergency comes, until self-preservation strikes its jarring gong — these are the features which constitute the endless repetition of history."

Your inaction as a writer means that you will repeat the same patterns that have stopped you from writing and completing projects, rewriting them, and ultimately sending them off to compete in the marketplace.

Ponder this thought: While you're busy not writing, thousands upon thousands of other writers are at their computers churning out pages. They may not be all that good, but these people are at least taking action, i.e., trying. And the more anyone tries, the more anyone writes, odds are they'll get better.

And if you don't get better, you'll have the satisfaction of knowing that you have tried.

Exercise

Make a list of all the ways you avoid writing, all the excuses you've come up with, all the lies you've told yourself, and all the people you've blamed for your lack of output.

> Read the list out loud.
> Then throw it away.
> Clean your work area.

The next morning, after you've showered and dressed, go to your computer and write something. Anything. A letter to someone you usually e-mail. Random thoughts on an old idea or new idea. Write about what you're feeling. Describe some long ago pleasant memory. Or an unpleasant one.

Just write with no desired outcome, other than to get your fingers typing, your brain thinking, and your body getting re-acclimated to the task of putting words on paper.

And if you don't have a comfortable writing chair, get one.

Character cannot be developed in ease and quiet. Only through experience of trial and suffering can the soul be strengthened, ambition inspired, and success achieved.

HELEN KELLER

STEP 10 | You continued to take personal inventory and when you were wrong about not taking constructive criticism and feedback you promptly admitted it to those who took the time to read your manuscript.

The Best Part of Doing Cocaine Is Going to Get It

Ask most cokeheads if the above statement is true and you'll get a resounding YES!

The excitement and anticipation is incredible, better than the high, which lasts only so long and has side effects like agitation, irritability, nervousness, or restlessness.

Oh yeah, and there's the expense. Let's not forget how much money a cokehead, rich or poor, dishes out for his nose candy.

Hmmm. Those sound like the side effects of not being able to write, of not being able to get your acts together. There are even financial consequences to not being able to write. How many Final Draft Screenwriting Program updates have you gone through? Plus the classes, books, magazine subscriptions, seminars, lectures, and computer upgrades?

You probably haven't spent as much as a coke-head, but there have been expenses.

If going to get cocaine is the best part of doing the drug, I submit that the best part of being a writer is getting a new idea. You've found a premise that you love. You've done an outline or some kind of cause-and-effect synopsis you're happy with, you've gotten positive feedback from someone you respect, and you're anxious to start.

It's a high!

Like a brand new relationship, all peachy and nice and fun until it stops being peachy and nice and fun. The high comes. The high goes. I'm sure you've gone through a few or at least one.

And just as any cokehead makes his score, gets high until it runs out and must place another or-der, such is the writer who gets his new idea and experiences the high of creativity until that high has evaporated and he's stuck with 42 pages of incoherent gibberish. Like the cokehead who calls his dealer for a new supply, the writer calls on his Muse for a new idea and the whole process starts all over again.

The relationship between a cokehead and his dealer is as codependent as they come. They say you know you're codependent when you're drowning and somebody else's life passes before your eyes. I believe we should become codependent with what we write by letting our characters, especially our protagonists, get into our heads. We can better focus on what a character wants, why he wants it, and what he must do to get it.

Just as a friend or therapist might ask a cokehead, "Why are you doing this to yourself?", a friend or therapist might ask a writer who isn't writing, "Why is this happening?"

Let's say it's you. Maybe you don't know. Maybe you've been asking yourself that question for months. Or years. Maybe, emotionally, you're incapable of answering the question.

Maybe your emotional skills are lacking or out of sync. This refers to one's ability to deal with, manage, express, and control his or her emotional states, including anger, sadness, excitement, anxiety, and joy. The simplest emotional vocabulary of all consists of four words for the four fundamental human emotions:

- SAD (forlorn, blue, gloomy)
- MAD (angry, irritable, furious)
- BAD (guilty, anxious, fearful)
- GLAD (happy, joyous, peaceful, content)

Although it's not clear that these four words cover all human emotions (experts say that surprise and disgust, for example, seem to be basic emotions that are not covered), they are nonetheless a very simple and easily understood cue for children to use to label their emotions.

Okay. Let's not talk about children.

How do *you* handle these four fundamental human emotions? Do you hide your sadness, anger, guilt, and/or happiness? And what about shame and hurt?

As a writer who can't get your acts together, do you allow yourself to feel sad when you're not writing? Do you get angry with yourself for avoiding your computer? Do you feel guilty or ashamed that you're so blocked you feel like you're in a state of limbo?

Or is it so bad that you feel as if an elephant is sitting on your chest and you can't breathe?

Do you feel happy that you've managed to get through a day without enduring the ineffable pain and frustration of not being able to write?

I'm going to guess that you never feel happy because you're not writing and you really want to write, so how can you be happy when the thing you want to do, *need* to do, isn't happening?

Maybe you're just relieved that you got through another 24 hours without having to stare at a blank monitor or page.

Maybe you've felt all of the above emotions at varying times of the day, week, month, or year. No matter what you do, you can't make it happen and you're stuck in a fog. Like the cokehead waiting for his dealer, anticipating the exchange of money for drugs, you're a writer waiting for your Muse to meet you with some inspiration.

If not a Muse, something. Anything that will get you back on track.

Again, the cokehead can go to rehab or a 12-Step Program and find help.

What can you do as a writer who's reached rock bottom? I suggest that you look at the other problems in your life and see if something (or more than one thing) is affecting your ability to write.

Money problems, relationship problems, job problems, et al. Something's preventing you from getting your nose to the grindstone and writing.

If you can't pinpoint the "other thing" that's stopping you from writing, it's time to get professional help.

You guessed it.

A shrink.

It may be your last resort.

Exercise

Writers aren't supposed to talk about what they're writing. Some say that by telling a friend the plot of your new script you're jinxing it.

You're "talking it away."

Some go so far as to say that your characters will become upset with you for talking about them, or the story they're in, and will punish you for doing so by not letting you write good dialogue for them. I believe that talking about what you're currently writing isn't healthy unless you're doing so in the context of asking for the advice of someone (usually another writer) on a problem you're having with a script.

But to just talk about what you're writing to anyone for the sake of bragging or getting attention is a no-no.

However, you can talk to yourself. Silently or out loud. I've found that by lying down or taking a walk, if I talk out my plot lines or character development, it helps. I mean, literally talking to myself about what a certain character wants or what his motivation is.

It can be surprisingly effective at getting the cobwebs out of your head, which will enable you to think clearly and enter a new gateway of creativity.

Remember, the lips that
are kissing your ass
are hiding teeth behind them.

PRABHUDOSS SAMUEL

STEP 11 | You sought through prayer and meditation to improve your conscious contact with God, as you understood Him, praying only for knowledge of His will for you and the power to carry that out by changing your disingenuous behavior and learning to get some backbone when dealing with agents, editors, managers, directors, and producers.

When People Pleasers Stop Pleasing People, People Aren't Pleased

Don't be so fucking nice. Nice is for dogs.

Don't be afraid to rock the boat. Boats in Hollywood, publishing, the theater and television were meant to be rocked.

Nobody in decision-making or buying positions respects you when you're too nice. They mistake it for weakness and they go in for the kill. These same people know it when someone is kissing their respective asses.

I've tried being nice and friendly and cooperative and all it ever got me was grief and, more importantly, no respect. I subconsciously (or maybe even consciously) sent a message that I could be pushed around. And not only by people older and more experienced than I, but younger as well.

If you're a screenwriter, the longer you climb the Hollywood mountain, the older you get and as the years build up, you'll find yourself having to deal with executives and industry people several (or many) years your junior. And don't forget that you'll be competing with screenwriters younger than you who are climbing the same mountain as you.

People with power, even a little, tend to lord it over the weak and as a new screenwriter (and not so new), you're the weakest one in the room.

Sure, you've written a screenplay that somebody is interested in, be it a producer, creative executive, or a studio. They like it enough to think about buying it and making it, but they don't like it enough to not want to mess with it.

And they will mess with it.

With rare exception, even established, successful screenwriters get their scripts fucked over.

The area of least resistance for most screenwriters is to take shit, hold your hat in your hand, smile like you're a slave on the plantation and do what the master tells you to.

I thought by being nice I was being cooperative and that it would get me closer to the deal. So I'd make changes to a script with great reluctance, changes that I knew were idiotic because I didn't want to rock the boat, i.e., screw up my deal.

People pleasing is a polite way to describe "ass kissing."

If you're going to kiss ass, make sure it's the right ass. As screenwriters, we are rarely above kissing the ass of the lowliest person in a production company if we think it will help us somehow.

People pleasers want everyone around them to be happy and they will do whatever is asked of them to keep it that way. What many people pleasers don't realize is that people pleasing can have serious risks. Not only does it put a lot of pressure and stress on you, it will bring your self-esteem down to the bottom.

In real life, people pleasers yearn for outside validation. They put everyone else before themselves. For some, saying "yes" is a habit; for others, it's almost an addiction that makes them feel that they need to be needed. This makes them feel important and as if they're contributing to someone else's life.

If you're a people-pleasing writer, you agree to things that producers, editors, creative executives, and directors say because you're petrified of not getting that deal that seems so close, or losing the deal that's so near to being sealed.

A people-pleasing writer will put up little or no resistance and that's when your downfall begins. Nobody likes a people pleaser, not really, because anyone with a brain knows that the people pleaser is really browning up to them to curry favor, or out of fear.

Any of this sound familiar?

How many times have you smiled awkwardly at someone showing interest in something you've written and agreed to make changes that would most likely make the project worse?

What kind of changes? Oh, stuff like...
- The ending.
- The beginning.
- The middle.
- Make the ending the beginning.
- Cut the middle out entirely and replace it with a subplot whose sole purpose is to attract an

up-and-coming actress who may attract the 12 to 24 demographic.

- Make your perfectly realized, extremely satisfying ending into something vague that makes no sense and will leave audiences scratching their heads as they leave the theater.
- Add a romantic subplot even though your screenplay is a drama about the last survivors of the Bubonic Plague.
- Delete a romantic subplot that ties everything together in the third act.
- Make a gay character not gay.
- Make your Caucasian protagonist African American, Turkish, Samoan, or an Eskimo.
- Cut all the hilarious lines because the wife of one of the producers doesn't get any of the jokes because she has no sense of humor, but thinks she does.

Anyway, you get the point.

People pleasing never gets a writer anything other than a bad feeling in the gut.

Please.

Stop the people pleasing already.

PLEASE!

Exercise

If you've been a people pleaser in the writing part of your life, you may also be one in other areas too. If you're going to change your behavior, the first step is to be aware that you're doing it.

Practice saying no. Don't be afraid to disagree with someone. Learn how to push back when you know in your heart you're being steamrolled or lied to.

Look backwards and try to develop an understanding as to when and why your people pleasing started. Therapy can be a tremendous help in this area.

*Our greatest weakness
lies in giving up.
The most certain way to
succeed is always to try
just one more time.*

THOMAS EDISON

STEP 12 | Having had a spiritual awakening as the result of these Steps, you tried to carry this message to other blocked, stymied, broken writers, and to practice these principles in all your affairs.

Hitting Bottom: Nothing Changes If Nothing Changes

You may not be an alcoholic, drug addict, or degenerate gambler, but something's going on in your head that's preventing you from being the writer you want to be.

You just can't get your act together.

You've probably hit bottom. How do you know?

You've lived with your non-writing/non-positive behavior for so long, made excuses to justify continuing along the same path, and generally convinced yourself and others that you can do what you want because it's your life.

The bottom is different for each person. Some writers throw in the towel after their first script. They've done everything right: sought out feedback, written several drafts, gotten it to a point where it's an excellent script. But they can't get an agent or manager to even look at it. They do what a first-time writer is supposed to do: write query letters and e-mails, ask everyone they know if they have a contact in the industry (however small), enter contests.

But, as the saying goes, they can't even get arrested.

"Everyone says my novel/screenplay/play/pilot is terrific!" they bemoan. "It's not fair. How come other people's inferior stuff gets sold and produced or published?"

The wailing and gnashing of teeth can go on for hours. For days. Not that the writer shouldn't allow himself some angry time. But when the angry time turns into bitter time and it lasts for weeks or months (or years) it crushes your soul.

I knew a young screenwriter who got a hotshot manager and sold a script while in grad school. He moved to Los Angeles and got a couple of writing assignments. He was succeeding. A few years passed and he continued to get deals and make money. But then the bullshit started. One of the scripts he sold (and was well paid for) got made, but by that time he was off the project and the script had been drastically rewritten. Another project got killed because of the unethical actions of another screenwriter, which tainted the project.

This screenwriter was in his late twenties. He couldn't take the bullshit any longer, walked away, returned to grad school, and pursued an entirely different career.

What may be the bottom for me may not be the same for you. Why is this? Because each human being has different belief sets (even a lack of religious belief is a belief set), varied backgrounds, education, family circumstances, financial status, jobs, goals (or lack of), and expectations (or not); the picture of the bottom will be different for everyone.

Most writers are in one kind of rut or another. It just ain't happening. You have a mediocre idea or not even an idea — maybe just a notion of a story. Or the premise you fell in love with doesn't love you back. It sounded like such a good idea at the time. Now you hate it and you wonder why you ever thought it was any good.

Back to the rut. You're not writing. The only thing you're doing is feeling sorry for yourself. Days go by. Maybe weeks. And then a few months have gone by and you're self-esteem is dwindling as your self-loathing is increasing.

That's when it really gets bad because you're starting to become immobilized with fear that you'll never find another good idea or that even if you do, you won't be able to finish a draft or, if you do, you won't be able to rewrite it or rethink it. That kind of thinking pushes you down even further into the miasma of a blocked writer.

Oh, by the way, that's what you've become. You are not a writer anymore. You are now a writer who can't break through his block and that's dangerous territory because with all that free time you have because you aren't writing, you can spend it "thinking" about how you're not writing and that brings you down even more.

Is there a way out of this horrible place?

Only if you change the course you've been on. How do you do that? Depends on your psyche. Maybe take a short vacation. Or a long one. Get away from your environment and the daily grind. Join a health club. Exercise can be a very freeing experience once you find a routine.

I won't kid you. There might be 50 things you can try to get away from your unproductive path and none of them may work. But you have to try.

If you don't, it'll only get worse. You have to change whatever pattern you've fallen into.

Because nothing changes if nothing changes, you have to take that first step.

There's no magic elixir to being a writer other than hard work. Once you've gotten yourself to sit down and begin writing, you're in the driver's seat, not your demons.

When you start a new project or go back to an older one, if you feel the onslaught of old doubts, fears, or misgivings, turn to the 12 Steps of *Writers Rehab* for sustenance.

Once you've taken that all-important first step, you'll find yourself swimming in different waters. Instead of being pulled down by the undercurrent of depression and anxiety, you now have the tools to stay afloat with a renewed sense of possibility.

Epilogue
For Comedy Writers,
Who Live in Their Own
Special Hell

Just as writing and completing a novel, play, screenplay, or television script is a slow, arduous process, getting your act together will also take time.

But once you've gotten yourself back on track you'll be ready for the next level.

I've used the foundational 12-step program of AA as the basis for *Writers Rehab*. In this final 13th Step, I do not have the audacity to try and improve on a system that has worked for so many people.

However, I submit this final step as a kind of bonus in appreciation of my fellow comedy writers who, besides struggling with all the complications of finishing a screenplay, novel, play, or teleplay, have the added burden of trying to be funny.

*Total absence of humor
renders life impossible.*

COLETTE

A Special STEP 13 for Writers of Comedy
You admitted to God, to yourself, and to fellow writers the exact nature of your inability to understand how to write a comedy, funny lines, comical situations, and comedic characters.

Comedy Writer: Heal Thyself!

Understand that comedy makes everything better. Chefs say that bacon makes everything they cook better. Comedy is like that too. Even the darkest, saddest drama needs a laugh or a light moment periodically, otherwise known as comic relief.

The classic Greek tragedies had one-liners. Elizabethan drama had the fool, the court jester.

Arthur Miller's play *Death of a Salesman* isn't a laugh a minute, but it's very funny, besides being one of the greatest American tragedies. David Mamet's tough-talking dramas like *Glengarry Glen Ross* and *Speed the Plow* are extremely funny.

Think of the darkest, most depressing movies you've ever seen and with rare exception there will be the occasional moment of humor. A character will say or do something that generates a laugh, a smile, or at least an appreciative nod.

Most of the comedy screenplays I read aren't funny enough or aren't funny at all. Paper-thin characters say supposedly funny lines that are stupid, stale, obvious, and easy. (There's nothing easier than writing a dick joke). Those same characters are in situations that, much of the time, are unbelievable. How many times have you watched a movie and thought to yourself, "I don't believe that."

Some might argue that it's a comedy and there doesn't have to be a lot of logic or situations based on reality. That might work on the lesser television sitcoms, but the best film comedies, certainly romantic comedies, are grounded in some semblance of how life really is.

Many comedies of the last decade are based around a premise and jokes are written to complement it rather than having a character in a comedic situation who must strive to get what he or she wants.

In the best-written comedies, the jokes and funny lines should come organically as the character moves towards his goal.

The question screenwriters of comedies need to ask themselves is: Where can I find fodder for humor? Where will I find the ideas for the lines I want a character to say and have an audience laugh at — and before that, have someone important read the script.

There are two ways:

You can look into your personal life and find material inspired by your friends, family, co-workers, girlfriends, boyfriends, wives, husbands, children, et al.

You can look beyond your own life and delve into the world of pop culture, personalities, politics, and celebrity.

Imagine yourself as a fly on the wall in the presence of famous people. Before their divorce, Ashton Kutcher tweeted a photo of Demi Moore in her underwear. What did she have to say about that? Before their divorce, Russell Brand tweeted a photo of Katy Perry without makeup. How'd she feel about that? Did either woman get upset? Did each of these couples have a huge fight? If so, what was that fight about? Both of those situations could inspire incredibly funny sketches.

These are just two instances that come to mind. Pick a personality or celebrity of your choice and imagine what goes on in his or her home behind closed doors.

What is it like to have been married to Rush Limbaugh? Wife No. 1 arrived when he was young and struggling. Wife No. 2 came along as his career took off. Wife No. 3 hit the jackpot. What would it be like if those three women got together and dished about life with Rush? He is currently on wife No. 4. What goes through her mind? Does she secretly wonder if she'll be his last wife? Does she ever want to talk to the other wives?

I can envision a funny bit: The Rush Limbaugh Ex-Wives Club. Or a parody of Limbaugh's ex-wives as Mormon sister wives.

Speaking of Mormons, Glenn Beck is a former Catholic who became a Mormon. When he was thinking of converting, did he call Donny Osmond, Rick Schroder, or Katherine Heigl to find out the pros and cons?

Speaking of right-wing conservatives, imagine what Glenn Beck and Rush Limbaugh would talk about if they ran into each other at a strip club. Awkward! But potentially funny.

When Kate Gosselin had her moment of fame and was left by her husband, was she petrified that she'd never find a man because she has eight kids? Who is her confidant? The woman who does her manicures? What would that conversation go like? Has she considered on-line dating? What qualities does she look for in a man? Must have had a vasectomy? Must have a low sperm count?

What is it like to be the personal assistant of Lindsay Lohan and what is on a typical To Do list for that assistant? Do Paul McCartney and Ringo Starr ever kid each other about which will be the last surviving Beatle? What would Simon Cowell and Steven Tyler text each other about?

Another problem with writing comedy is accepting criticism.

If you're new to comedy writing one of the biggest hurdles you'll have to face is criticism. You probably know what it's like to tell a joke or toss off an ad-lib and get a blank stare. Everyone does. But most people aren't comedy writers, so if they fail at saying something funny they can shrug it off and forget about it.

But if you're writing a screenplay that's a comedy you're not in a position to shrug off the fact that the three people you gave your script to for feedback all said that it wasn't funny; you need to pay attention.

Your first reaction will usually be anger. You've convinced yourself that what you wrote is funny. You've done four drafts. Every time you read it you laugh. You just *know* it's hilarious.

Frankly, you're too close to it. You need two things: distance and some honest feedback.

For comedy writers the harshest form of criticism is when nobody's laughing (or not enough people are laughing). In a typical comedy writing class there might be anywhere from 10 to 15 people working on screenplays or sitcom spec scripts. Let's say you're in that class. If you bring in the first few scenes of your new romantic comedy and everybody's laughing it means what you've written is funny.

If only one person is laughing it means it's not funny. And perhaps that one person laughing is your friend so it doesn't count. Or maybe the one person laughing only laughed out of pity.

Learn this now: There's nothing worse than a pity laugh.

Learn this too: Stay clear of people who are too kind in their criticism. You want truth tellers reading your screenplays. People who say "I like it a lot" or "It's really funny" or whatever polite line of bull they blurt out aren't helping you. The person who tells you that she didn't laugh much or that a character's lines are tasteless, offensive, sexist, gross, and immature is your friend.

Let's return to the aforementioned comedy writing class. Problems arise when half the class is laughing and the other half isn't. Why are seven or eight people laughing hysterically at the same scene, while the rest of the class is sitting there, unsmiling and rolling their eyes, clearly not getting it?

If there's a rational answer, it's differing sensibilities. To some, nothing is sacred. To others, certain subjects are very sacred and untouchable. Some have a perpetual frat boy sensibility in which bodily function humor, gross behavior, and dick jokes rule. Then there are those who've "grown up" and prefer a more adult, witty, clever type of situation and dialogue.

When you sit at your computer writing funny dialogue it may genuinely be very funny. You may be laughing as the words pour onto the page. Or when you sit back and read what you've written, again, you may break yourself up.

You might also be setting yourself up.

Clever, witty, funny dialogue is deceptive. Sometimes you can be too clever. Too esoteric. I always encourage comedy writers to be smart and current with what's going on in the world. But sometimes being too smart/clever/esoteric won't work to your advantage.

When I read a comedy I *want* to laugh. Give me at least one laugh per page. Three, four, or five is even better. As the saying goes, "Keep 'em coming."

Listen to the people who are reading your script. Try to get as much specific feedback as possible as to what isn't working for them humor-wise.

....

I know a lot of comedy writers.

Some are funnier than others both in daily life and on the page. More often than you'd imagine, the funniest scripts are written by men and women who aren't that much fun to be around. They can "write" funny, but not "be" very funny during normal life. Some are downright boring while others are depressed and a drag to be around.

Ironically, some of the funniest people I know are hilarious when they're hanging out with friends or one-on-one, but they aren't funny on paper. Because they were so funny, early in their careers they tried writing comedy, but they realized after a few not-very-laugh-filled scripts that comedy wasn't their forte.

They shut the door on writing comedy and found their niche elsewhere.

But that doesn't apply to someone who can actually write funny stuff.

Let's say that's you.

In my experience as a writer and teacher, I've learned that some comedy writers (like some people) are naturally funny while others have to work at it.

Think back to your childhood. Remember the boy who was the class clown? (It was pretty much always a boy. Funny girls were considered to be weird. And guys, how intimidated are you by a witty, funny woman?) He irritated the teacher and generated giggles from classmates not so much by making witty remarks, but mainly by doing goofy stuff, making faces, and pulling off slap-sticky things.

I went through each year of grade school with the same group of kids. There were the smart kids (not me), the athletes (not me), the cool kids (definitely not me), the outcasts (fortunately not me: that was to come during high school), the gen-pop (kids who were just there, usually well behaved and religious) and the two kids competing to be class clown (one of which was me).

Competing is a generous word. There was no competition. The other kid, Joey, was hands down the funniest kid in class. I was a distant second. *Really* distant. Looking back, kids laughed *at* me more than because of something funny I did or said.

Joey was cute and had a killer smile. I was kind of geeky-looking and when I smiled my face wrinkled up in a way that made me look as if I had progeria (a rare abnormality marked by premature aging, grey hair, wrinkled skin, and stooped posture in a child). Joey was charming. I wasn't. All the girls had crushes on him and all the boys wanted to either hang with him or *be* him.

Nobody wanted to be me. *I* didn't even want to be me.

What I wanted was to make my classmates laugh (attention, duh!). The problem was that Joey was a natural. I wasn't. He would open his mouth and most of the time something clever came out. And when what he said missed the mark, he had learned to ignore it and move on to the next ad lib.

I didn't know what an ad-lib was. I didn't know what being witty or clever meant.

At some point, I started to realize that, unlike Joey, I would have to work at getting laughs.

Work very hard!

Which brings us back to comedy writing.

At some point you decided that you wanted to be a comedy writer. For me, it was in my early twenties. I started out writing plays, specifically, comedies.

That is when I realized that my writing career was a re-creation of my childhood desire to be class clown. Instead of competing with one Joey who didn't have to work that hard at getting laughs, I would be competing with lots of Joeys to whom comedy writing came, if not "easy," certainly "easier."

Being a comedy writer isn't just a matter of writing funny dialogue, bits, or set pieces. There's a whole other level to confuse you.

What kind of comedy do you write?

You're at a party, in a bar, or somewhere and you're talking with someone you just met. You let it slip that you're a screenwriter and the person asks you what kind of stuff you write.

Someone who doesn't write comedies might answer without a moment's hesitation in the following way:

"I write — "Thrillers. Action. Sci-Fi. Adventure. Mysteries. Indies. Horror. Drama."

These writers are lucky. They know their identity as a screenwriter.

But if you're a comedy writer your answer might not come as easily.

What would your answer be? That you write: Comedies? Comedy/dramas? Serio/comedies? Dramadies? Dramatic comedies? Romantic comedies? Buddy comedies? Bittersweet comedies? Comedy/adventures? Sex comedies? Dark comedies? Farce? Parody?

Pinpointing the type of comedies you write is important, especially if the person who asked what kind of screenplays you write is an agent, manager, producer, development executive, or somebody in the business who might help you.

The industry is constantly changing. Knowing the kind of comedy you write is a way of creating your brand. Maybe the old school term for branding is just as good: *pigeonholed.*

In television you're either a sitcom writer or you write hour-long drama. You might eventually do both, but you'll break into the business as one or the other.

Before Alan Ball wrote *Six Feet Under* and *True Blood*, he wrote for *Grace Under Fire* and *Cybill*. He made the transition, which also included a little detour into screenwriting called *American Beauty*. Same with Terence Winter. Before he wrote for *The Sopranos* and created *Boardwalk Empire* he wrote for *Flipper* and *Sister, Sister*.

Judd Apatow is known for a certain kind of comedy. So are Nancy Meyers and the late Nora Ephron. So are the Farrelly brothers, Adam Sandler, Diablo Cody, Kevin Smith, and Dana Fox.

Woody Allen is in a genre-bending league all his own. There are four stages of his career. (1) Fun, goofy comedies: *Bananas*, *Take the Money and Run*, and *Sleeper*. (2) Comedy/dramas: *Annie Hall*, *Manhattan*, and *Broadway Danny Rose*. (3) Dramatic/comedies: *Stardust Memories*, *Crimes and Misdemeanors*, *Radio Days*. (4) This is the most difficult to pinpoint. Even diehard Woody Allen fans, of which I am one, have found his output over the last 15 years to be inconsistent. His films are a mix of comedy/dramas and dramadies (*Midnight in Paris, Deconstructing Harry, Match Point, Vicky Cristina Barcelona, Whatever Works*). His lesser successes are more difficult to pinpoint (*Anything Else, Cassandra's Dream, You Will Meet a Tall Dark Stranger, To Rome with Love*).

Now we should all be so lucky to have careers as long and productive as Woody Allen's. Even if his best work is behind him, he leaves a tremendous legacy. I bring him up simply to illustrate that though he began his screenwriting career writing lowbrow comedies he aspired to greater heights and achieved them. As of this writing he's authored more than 40 screenplays.

What about you? You're writing comedies. Are you able to narrow them down to the kind you write? It's important to your career that you know, so when someone who can help you asks what you write you can be specific.

But maybe you don't know your genre of comedy or you're not sure. You may still be finding your voice.

Do you want to be known as the screenwriter who writes raunchy, vulgar, stupid stuff (that might get you a huge deal and a house in Malibu) or do you want to be known as the writer of witty, clever, smart comedies? The kind that gets nominated for Academy Awards.

The ability to write raunchy comedies and dick jokes is a certain kind of talent that might get you in the door. If you're relatively young, your life experience might still be in the adolescent/frat-boy vein. You can outgrow that if you choose. Maybe you won't want to. Maybe that's all you're capable of. If that's the case, you'll be branded as a one-trick pony.

But as you get older you might want to change your professional image. Woody Allen came a long way from *Bananas* to *Crimes and Misdemeanors*. But if you start out wanting to write comedies that are grounded in reality and filled with wit and intelligence, you'll be positioning yourself on a higher plain.

You'll be the comedy screenwriter others aspire to be.

And that's nothing to laugh about!

About the Author | D.B. Gilles

D.B. Gilles teaches screenwriting and comedy writing in The Maurice Kanbar Institute of Film & Television at New York University's Tisch School of the Arts. He has also taught in the Graduate Film Department at Columbia University, the Department of

Photo courtesy of Allison Maggy

Dramatic Writing at NYU where he taught playwriting, and The Gallatin School of Individualized Study at NYU.

His fiction includes the comic novel *I Hate My Book Club* and the mystery *Colder Than Death*. Several plays he wrote have been produced and published, most notably *Men's Singles*, *The Girl Who Loved the Beatles* and *Inadmissible*.

He is the author of *The Screenwriter Within* (2nd Ed.): *New Strategies to Finish Your Screenplay & Get a Deal!*; *You're Funny! Turn Your Sense of Humor Into a Lucrative New Career*; and *The Portable Film School*.

He is also one of the most in-demand script consultants and writing coaches in the country, working with screenwriters, novelists, television writers and playwrights.

Contact the Author

D.B. Gilles

Interface with D.B. Gilles directly.
Google his Blog—Writers Rehab

For other books by D.B. Gilles go to
http://dbgillesbooks.blogspot.com

Twitter: @dbgilles

http://www.facebook.com/dbgilles

For Script Consultation contact
D.B. Gilles at:
dbgillescript@gmail.com

YOU'RE FUNNY!
TURN YOUR SENSE OF HUMOR
INTO A LUCRATIVE NEW CAREER

D.B. GILLES

You're Funny! is the next best thing to being in a comedy writing
class. It covers the different ways to earn a living as a comedy
writer, including writing sitcoms, jokes for late night talk shows,
parody, stand up, and screenwriting and will help you deter-
mine if you can actually make a living writing jokes and making
people laugh.

*"Fast. Funny. Informative. D.B. Gilles has written a delightful
book about tapping into your inner funny. Read it. You'll laugh.
You'll learn."*

> — Matt Williams, co-creator/producer, *Roseanne*,
> *Home Improvement*; director, *Where The Heart Is*

*"D.B. is a positive force for comedy. This book is a funny, entertaining, and practical guide for
anyone wanting to break into the world of comedy writing."*

> — Jeff Cox, writer, *Blades of Glory*

*"You're Funny! is one of the best books available on comedy writing with a 24 carat gold payoff-
specific guidance on how to turn those skills into a profitable career."*

> — Don DeMaio, teacher, American Comedy Institute, NYC

*"You're Funny! is the first how-to handbook that ever got me laughing out loud. A long-time
student of the comedy game, D.B. knows his stuff and is damned funny in passing the secrets
on. A real treat."*

> — David McKenna, co-author of *Memo From The Story Department*

D.B. GILLES has taught comedy writing and screenwriting in the Undergraduate Film & Television
Department at New York University's Tisch School of the Arts for nearly 20 years. He is the author
of *The Screenwriter Within: How to Turn The Movie in Your Head Into a Salable Screenplay* and
The Portable Film School. He is co-author of the George Bush parody *W. The First Hundred Days:
A White House Journal.* D.B. is also a script consultant and writing coach. He writes the popular
blog *Screenwriters Rehab: For Screenwriters Who Can't Get Their Acts Together.* His new play
Sparkling Object opened last year in New York.

$19.95 · 185 PAGES · ORDER NUMBER 160RLS · ISBN: 9781932907957

THE SCREENWRITER WITHIN - 2ND ED.
NEW STRATEGIES TO FINISH YOUR SCREENPLAY & GET A DEAL!

D.B. GILLES

The hardest thing about screenwriting is completing it. At last — a way to do this! The second edition of *The Screenwriter Within* is like having D.B. Gilles as your personal career coach. He specializes in motivating screenwriters to rethink, rewrite, and complete their scripts and bringing them closer to a deal and money in their pockets.

"My God, he's done it! D.B. Gilles has topped himself. I previously felt nothing can be better than his first book on screenwriting. D.B. now comes out with the second edition of The Screenwriter Within. *Better wisdom, laughs, and heart!"*

— Dr. Lew Hunter, screenwriter, author of *Lew Hunter's Screenwriting 434*, Chairman, UCLA Screenwriting Department

"The 2nd edition of Screenwriter Within *is just as knowledgeable and fun as D.B.'s screenwriting classes, with real-world insights into the life of a professional writer and working in Hollywood."*

— David Benullo, writer, *Around the World in 80 Days*, *The Dead Zone*

"The wisest, funniest, most grounded-in-reality screenwriting coach you can imagine... a lifetime's worth of insider tips and common-sense strategies for mastering the screenwriting game."

— Christopher Vogler, author, *The Writer's Journey*; co-author, *Memo from the Story Dept.*

"You won't find a better book that focuses on the basics (and more) than The Screenwriter Within, 2nd Edition. *Written with humor, honesty and clarity — it will truly help you improve your screenplay."*

— Matthew Terry, filmmaker; screenwriter; teacher; columnist for www.hollywoodlitsales.com

D.B. GILLES has taught screenwriting and comedy writing in the Undergraduate Film & Television Department at New York University's Tisch School of the Arts for nearly 20 years. He is the author of *You're Funny! Turn Your Sense of Humor Into a Lucrative New Career* and *The Portable Film School*. He is co-author of the George Bush parody *W. The First Hundred Days, A White House Journal*. D.B. is also a Script Consultant and Writing Coach. He writes the popular blog, *Screenwriters Rehab: For Screenwriters Who Can't Get Their Acts Together*. His new play *Sparkling Object* opened in New York, Fall 2010. He is a member of The Writers Guild of America.

$22.95 · 250 PAGES · ORDER NUMBER 169RLS · ISBN: 9781615930579

THE MYTH OF MWP

In a dark time, a light bringer came along, leading the curious and the frustrated to clarity and empowerment. It took the well-guarded secrets out of the hands of the few and made them available to all. It spread a spirit of openness and creative freedom, and built a storehouse of knowledge dedicated to the betterment of the arts.

The essence of the Michael Wiese Productions (MWP) is empowering people who have the burning desire to express themselves creatively. We help them realize their dreams by putting the tools in their hands. We demystify the sometimes secretive worlds of screenwriting, directing, acting, producing, film financing, and other media crafts.

By doing so, we hope to bring forth a realization of 'conscious media' which we define as being positively charged, emphasizing hope and affirming positive values like trust, cooperation, self-empowerment, freedom, and love. Grounded in the deep roots of myth, it aims to be healing both for those who make the art and those who encounter it. It hopes to be transformative for people, opening doors to new possibilities and pulling back veils to reveal hidden worlds.

MWP has built a storehouse of knowledge unequaled in the world, for no other publisher has so many titles on the media arts. Please visit www.mwp.com where you will find many free resources and a 25% discount on our books. Sign up and become part of the wider creative community!

Onward and upward,

Michael Wiese
Publisher/Filmmaker